Lucid D

Acquire Expertise In Experiencing The Separation Of
Consciousness From The Physical Body In Higher
Dimensions Through The Practice Of Astral Projection

*(Mastering Dream Control And Achieving Lucidity During
Sleep)*

JacBoogaard

TABLE OF CONTENT

Advanced Methods For Lucid Dreaming

As you gain more lucid dreaming experience, you might want to look into more sophisticated methods to improve your dream experiences. Try these advanced methods that are listed below:

Dream stabilization: It can be difficult to remain lucid and stay in a dream for a long time once you become lucid. You can extend the duration of your dream experience and preserve lucidity with dream stabilization techniques. You can stay in the dream by using techniques like circling, rubbing your hands together, or focusing on an object in the dream.

Dream manipulation: You can change the course of a dream to fit your desires if you are conscious during the dream. For instance, you can alter the dream's setting, cast of characters, and even the laws of physics. Pushing the envelope of what is possible and exploring the dream world can be done excitingly and engagingly like this.

Devices for inducing lucid dreams: A number of tools are available to assist in achieving lucid dreams. These gadgets include lucid dream masks, which alert the dreamer to the fact they are dreaming by producing light and sound cues, and lucid dream supplements, intended to improve dream memory and lucidity.

Reality checks: These techniques can help you become aware of your dreams. These self-checks can involve checking whether you're awake, feeling through your palm with your finger, or searching for dream symbols. You can raise your chances of being lucid and becoming more conscious of your dream state by including reality checks in your routine.

Experimentation and exploration: As your lucid dreaming skills improve, you can use them to explore the dream world in novel and fascinating ways. In your dreams, you can teleport, fly, or even travel through time. A fun and fascinating method to experience lucid dreaming is to experiment with various techniques and explore the dream world.

It's critical to remember that learning to achieve lucid dreaming requires patience and effort. You will eventually see progress if you persist and don't notice results immediately. Additionally, remember that each person has a different dream experience, so don't hesitate to try different things until you find what works best for you.

To sum up, sophisticated, lucid dreaming methods can improve your dream experiences and let you discover the dream world in novel and fascinating ways. You can lengthen your dream experience and increase your awareness of the dream state by using techniques like dream stabilization, manipulation, lucid dream induction devices, reality checks, and exploration and experimentation. Recall that mastering lucid dreaming is a process that requires time and effort, so don't give up if you don't notice results right away. With persistence, you will eventually make progress. Since every person has a different dream experience, don't be scared to try different things until you find what works best for you.

Chapter 10: Wrap-Up and Additional Resources

In this book, we have explored the intriguing field of lucid dreaming and how it might enhance our lives. We've talked about the science of dreams, how to induce lucid dreams, how to traverse the dream world and use it for self-discovery and personal growth, and how to overcome anxieties and nightmares.

A potent tool for self-awareness and personal growth is lucid dreaming. It enables us to take charge of our ambitions and utilize them to conquer obstacles, find solutions to issues, and accomplish our objectives. It also gives us a distinctive viewpoint on the ideas and emotions in our subconscious, which is incredibly helpful for personal development and self-discovery.

However, it's crucial to remember that learning to achieve lucid dreaming requires time and effort. It's a process rather than an event. If you keep trying and don't see results immediately, you'll eventually figure out what works best for you. Don't give up. Also, improve your ability to have lucid dreams.

Many resources are accessible for people who want to learn more about lucid dreaming. In addition to a plethora of knowledge available through books, articles, and websites, meet people interested in lucid dreaming. Furthermore, there are training courses, seminars, and workshops that can aid in developing your lucid dreaming abilities and offer direction and encouragement.

Stages Of Sleep

Understanding the normal sleep rhythms of the human brain can help us understand how and when dreams happen. They're sometimes referred to as sleep stages or cycles. Dream studies in the lab are made possible by scientists and psychologists who thoroughly understand each Stage and how different brain waves function during each.

This information can determine when dreams happen during your sleep cycle. With this information, you may arrange your sleep routine to maximize the likelihood that you will remember your dreams, including when to wake up. Additionally, you will be able to use the methods that can assist you in having a lucid dream and establish the ideal setting to increase your chances of having one. The following chapter will go over these. Understanding how a sleep cycle functions can also help you fall asleep if a dream wakes you up in the middle of the night. You'll discover how simple it is to fall back asleep. Here, the stages of sleep and their attributes are described for you with minimal scientific jargon, along with explanations of pertinent technical details.

You go through five stages when you sleep, labeled stages I through IV in Roman numerals. The fifth and final Stage is called REM sleep, or rapid eye movement sleep. Different levels of respiration, eye movement, and brain wave patterns are involved in each step. It's interesting to note that a person does not always start in Stage I when they first fall asleep, as you may have encountered at some point in your life. If you're someone who usually burns the candle at both ends, you might discover that as soon as you lay down, you fall asleep quickly. When someone is tired (such as shift workers, students, or workaholics), they may almost instantly enter the deep, dream stage of sleep. This sleep cycle organization is more common among those who work long hours and spend little time sleeping between work sessions, anywhere from 30 minutes to several hours.

● Stage I: This is when most people fall asleep because it marks the start of the sleep cycle. In Stage I sleep, a person is in a semi-conscious condition that makes it easy to rouse them up. The sense that one is beginning to fall asleep and the slow eye movement are signs of light sleep. Additionally, beta waves are still present here but are starting to diminish. The quickest brain wave type we often use to digest large amounts of information during the day is the beta wave. During this phase, the activity of alpha waves, which are a little slower than beta waves, increases.

● Stage II: At this point, the eyeballs stop moving. An increase in alpha-wave activity promotes deeper rest. Though they still exhibit sporadic spikes in activity known as sleep spindles, beta waves' activity is still declining.

● Stage III: At this Stage, brain waves are significantly slower. Alpha and theta waves, even slower than alpha waves, take center Stage as the beta wave function fades to the background. It is thought that theta waves connect the subconscious and conscious minds. Research on brain waves has also demonstrated that devoted practitioners of deep meditation, including yogis and Buddhist monks, exhibit higher theta wave activity when awake and during meditation. There is also an intermingling of delta waves, indicative of a deep sleep pattern.

● Phase IV: The brain emits just delta waves during this period. This is the most profound sleep stage associated with an unconscious mental state. Individuals who sleep like bears are extremely accustomed to this state and are not bothered by mild stimuli, save for sudden, loud, or violently startled awake. This phase is crucial since the body secretes the hormones that allow for adult body regeneration, repair, and new growth in children and teenagers. If you are experiencing chronic pain or exhaustion, it is most likely due to poor sleep quality and little to no time spent in Stage IV sleep.

● Rapid, shallow, erratic breathing characterizes REM sleep. The name implies that there is also a very quick movement of the eyes beneath closed lids. Other body parts, such as the limbs, typically have no muscle activity. Blood pressure and heart rate are getting close to waking levels. Dreams also happen during this phase. While theta and alpha waves do return to prominence, alpha waves are more prevalent during REM sleep.

People go through the five stages during a night's sleep before beginning at Stage I. A sleep cycle takes roughly 90 to 100 minutes to finish, while the length of time in each Stage varies depending on the time of night. Stated differently, an individual spends most of the night in Stage I and REM sleep toward the morning and more time in stages III and IV toward the night's start. An adult can spend 20% to 25% of the night in the REM state, 50% of the time in state II, and 30% of the time in the other stages of sleep when their sleep stages are balanced.

Since a sleep cycle takes a while to finish, you can usually arrange your schedule such that you wake up just as the REM state is about to begin. If you believe you don't usually remember dreams, this technique will increase your chances. If you do this, you'll have a higher chance of remembering the specifics of your dreams if you typically struggle to recall them. If you intend to go to bed at 10 p.m., for instance, you may set an alarm for approximately 4 a.m., 5:30, 7 a.m., or 8:30 p.m. to ensure that you are in the REM state. The time between when you go to sleep and the start of the first cycle must be calculated and scheduled. Following that, each cycle should take ninety to one hundred minutes to complete. The following lucid dreaming chapter will explain how psychologists do this type of research in dream laboratories. Give it some time and try again if your initial attempt at this experiment fails. Your odds of capturing a dream, recording it, and examining its contents rise with each attempt.

On a related note, you can wake up in the middle of the night from a dream that has disturbed your sleep. Depending on your typical sleep routine, your stress level, and the dream you experienced, you can find it difficult to fall back asleep. If this is the case, it is beneficial to discuss some of it.

Keep a notebook close to your bed so you may quickly jot down any memories of your dream. By putting it in writing, you'll be able to go over it later and avoid having to spend the night thinking back on your dream. Similarly, if the dream caused you to feel strongly emotionally, journaling about it will help you let go of those emotions rather than letting them fester and keep you from falling back asleep.

If you think, "Oh no, I can't sleep again now that I'm up," remember that you have just exited the final phase of your sleep cycle. This implies that you will inherently feel more alert and that your body might sense it is time to wake up. Your brain is about to enter beta wave mode, characterized by rapid, active information processing. In addition, if it is starved, it will fend for itself by searching through your schedule and to-do lists for outdated issues or information it can analyze. This is the main cause of your inability to get back asleep. When this occurs, your brain can be tricked.

How can you transition smoothly into the next sleep cycle after finishing the previous one? Take a seat up in bed for a little. Start breathing rhythmically and gradually deepen to moderately. Remember that rapid, shallow breathing during REM sleep lowers oxygen levels in your body and brain. That element may keep you from feeling completely at ease. This component of the innate process makes it possible for you to wake up in the first place.

Rise slowly after a minute or two of finding a steady, comfortable breathing pattern. Maintain a steady breathing pattern while performing a few basic stretches. For a nice stretch, raise your arms above your head, lean forward and try to touch your toes, etc. Your brain activity will slightly decrease because it will believe that you are getting ready for the day. You will have avoided the effects of your brain's innate urge to return to full wakefulness up to this point. Now close your eyes and take in the room's darkness. Tell yourself that it's still nighttime, soften your stare and that you're going back to bed. Look at your bed and mentally note how comfortable it looks. Once again, take slow, steady breaths before getting back into bed. Take solace in the warmth from cuddling into your pillow and beneath the covers and blanket. Shut your eyes and promise yourself you're going back to sleep. Pay attention to the calm, deep breaths you're taking. You ought to be able to return to Stage I sleep, characterized by semi-consciousness, soon.

Methods of Inducing Lucidity in Chapter 6

Gaining control over the dream state requires first achieving clarity in your dreams. Three of the best methods for achieving lucidity will be discussed in this chapter: presleep visualization, wake-back-to-bed (WBTB), and mnemonically induced lucid dream (MILD).

Mnemonically Induced Lucid Dream (MILD): This method entails consciously remembering that you are dreaming before you go to sleep. The goal is to sow the seed in your consciousness to identify the dream state as soon as it materializes. To apply this method, just tell yourself, "I will remember that I am dreaming," multiple times before bed.

Method of Wake-Back-to-Bed (WBTB): The WBTB approach calls for returning to bed right away after waking up for a few hours. This method may be useful because it raises the likelihood of going into the rapid eye movement (REM) sleep state when dreaming is most likely to happen. Affirmations or visualizations that support your aim to become lucid in dreams should be repeated before you turn in for the night.

Visualization of Presleep: Visualizing yourself becoming lucid in your dreams before going to sleep is known as presleep visualization. Using this technique, you can help sow the seed of lucidity in your mind and raise your chances of experiencing lucid dreams. Begin by imagining yourself in a scenario where you realize you are dreaming and go through the feelings of being in a dream.

In conclusion, lucidity in dreams can be induced using these three strategies. You can raise your chances of reaping the benefits of lucid dreaming by implementing one or more of these approaches into your dream practice.

The science of sleep, including its stages, the function of the brain, and the effects of sleep deprivation on dream experiences, will be discussed in the upcoming chapter. Gaining knowledge about the science underlying the dream state might help you better grasp this potent conscious state and offer insightful information on the lucidity induction procedure.

The Study Of Dreams And Sleep Science

Dreaming and sleeping are normal, physiological processes vital to our physical and emotional well-being. The stages of sleep, the brain's function, and the effects of sleep deprivation on dream experiences will all be covered in this chapter's scientific examination of the dream state and sleep cycle.

Sleeping phases: Five sleep phases are characterized by unique brainwave patterns and physiological alterations. DreamingDreaming is most likely to happen, which characterizes the fifth sleep stage, distinguished by slow wave (or non-REM) sleep. The brain is busy during REM sleep, resulting in vivid and creative dreams.

The Brain's Role: The brain is essential to sleep, dreaming, and transitioning between sleep stages. It also controls the Creation of dream imagery. Three important brain regions—the brainstem, hypothalamus, and thalamus—control sleep and dreaming. These regions collaborate with the cortex, the brain's outer layer, to generate the sensory experiences of dreaming.

Effects of Sleep loss: Sleep loss can significantly impact the quantity and quality of dreams. We are more likely to have trouble getting and staying asleep when we are sleep-deprived, which may lead to fewer possibilities for dream recall and less vivid dreams. Lack of sleep can also affect how emotions are regulated, which can exacerbate feelings of stress, anxiety, and sadness.

In summary, various brain regions and physiological systems manage the intricate processes of sleep and dreaming. Knowledge about the science underlying sleep and the dream state can help you improve your comprehension of this potent conscious state and offer insightful information about the possible advantages of lucid dreaming.

We will discuss dream recall in the upcoming chapter, along with its significance, methods for enhancement, and the advantages of dream journaling. By strengthening your dream memory, you can raise your odds of experiencing lucidity and learn more about your dream experiences.

Here's how to apply the WBTB technique step-by-step:

First, set an alarm.

Before bed, schedule an alarm for four to six hours later. This is important because it usually marks the conclusion of a deep sleep cycle and the start of the REM sleep phase when dreams are most vivid and unforgettable.

Step 2: Get out of bed and wake up

Wake up and get out of bed when your alarm goes off. You must get out of bed and move about to awaken your body and mind.

Step 3: Take part in a low-impact exercise

Take 15 to 30 minutes to do something low-key, peaceful, and devoid of bright lights or screens. This might be as simple as thinking about your goals for lucid dreaming, reading a book, or practicing meditation. It's important to keep your mind active but not overstimulated because it can make falling back asleep harder.

Step 4: Go back to sleep and concentrate on your goals
Once you've had a little time to wake up, go back to bed and go over your goals for lucid dreaming in your mind. This is the ideal time to go through the MILD steps and picture yourself lucid in a dream if you combine WBTB with the MILD technique.

Step 5: Go back to sleep
Keep your lucid dreaming intentions front and center as you drift back to sleep. This will raise the possibility of lucid dreams during the subsequent REM sleep cycle and assist in preparing your mind to identify when you're dreaming.

The WBTB method can be quite successful, but its results can change from night to night. Should you discover that WBTB significantly disturbs your sleep or makes it tough to get back asleep, you might need to modify the technique's timing or frequency to fit your unique sleep schedule better.

Since you're new to lucid dreaming, I strongly advise you to become proficient in MILD before using the WBTB method. This is because using the WBTB approach to its full potential can require recognizing dream indicators and conducting reality checks, both of which MILD helps to establish. Furthermore, MILD can help you improve your dream recall and raise your awareness of dreams, which is essential for reaching lucidity. Allow me to tell you another tale about that friend from college I told you about. He utilized reality checks to have his first lucid dream. After his first success, he was keen to investigate other methods of inducing lucid dreams, so he attempted the WBTB approach. But he soon found that because he wasn't quite comfortable with the MILD technique, adding WBTB to his practice was difficult.

My acquaintance first had trouble focusing intensely on his goals for lucid dreaming when he woke up in the middle of the night and went back to sleep. Frequently, he would find himself too alert to drift back to sleep or too disoriented to focus on his goals. As a result, there were multiple sleepless nights and no vivid dreams. He contacted me for help since he was frustrated, and I advised him to examine his strategy more carefully and think about concentrating on MILD before pursuing WBTB.

My friend decided to stand back and concentrate on becoming an expert in the MILD technique after realizing he needed to improve his strategy. He worked hard for several weeks, honing his reality checks, practicing MILD, and improving his dream recall. Additionally, he experimented with several mental exercises to help him focus on his goals and maintain his attention in the critical moments before going to sleep. In this period, my friend also turned to online lucid dreaming communities for guidance and support, where he met people who had gone through comparable struggles. He learned a great deal about the subtleties of MILD and useful tips and tactics that improved his skills from these exchanges.

He decided to give WBTB another shot when he was comfortable with his MILD skills. This time, he discovered that the mix of WBTB and MILD was far more successful. He noted a marked rise in the frequency and vividness of his lucid dreams, in addition to having an easier time going back to sleep with a clear concentration on his aims. Looking back, he saw that his success with the WBTB technique had largely depended on his taking the time to perfect MILD first.

This should serve as a reminder to you of how crucial it is to establish a strong foundation in lucid dreaming techniques prior to attempting more complex approaches. Potential obstacles and raise your chances of consistently having fulfilling lucid dreams by learning MILD first and implementing WBTB afterward. So, ensure you fully understand MILD and the fundamentals of lucid dreaming before plunging into the world of WBTB. You'll be glad you took the time and tried to establish this foundation for yourself later on.

As with any new ability or practice, learning to produce lucid dreams with the MILD approach can initially present difficulties. These early challenges are typical and can be ascribed to several things, including inexperience, unfamiliarity with the method, or just getting used to integrating lucid dreaming exercises into one's everyday schedule.
It's crucial to remember that getting past these obstacles is a normal part of learning. If you have the right patience, persistence, and willingness to

troubleshoot and improve your strategy, you should have more regular and vivid lucid dreams.

Girlfriend-Lady

I had my first major metamorphosis a few years following my college graduation. I went on a date that day with a stunning young woman I had met on a train a few weeks before. We had previously had sex on our third date, so I didn't think there was anything to be concerned about. However, I was mistaken when she turned up with a different man.

I believed she had double-dated herself because we were in a downtown Manhattan restaurant that I liked for its great seafood variety, easy location, and calm atmosphere. I had no idea what to anticipate, but she acted with such admirable confidence that she walked to my table with her buddy following closely after. She sat in front of me with such determination in her eyes. The man took a chair and sank next to her, their backs to me and my legs comfortable extending past theirs without coming into contact with theirs.

I didn't say anything while she described her turbulent connection with this man, whose name I usually manage to forget. I was listening and trying to comprehend her. My cunning date was gorgeous—no older than thirty—with naturally blonde hair and a figure so trim I could have spent the entire day holding her in my arms. Not only did she have a better appearance than everybody else, but she also had that unique quality that made me fall in love with her. She was almost that unicorn, the one with magical powers, who got lost in the harsh realities of Creation and found herself in a harshly unsuitable world for her delicate disposition. He was not, however, the man. I initially believed him to be a handy friend she had put in a more heroic role for a short while. However, then I saw the distinct expression in his eyes, the look of a coward in over his head while trying to play it cool, and I realized that he had already closed on this woman, though I could not imagine how. He was unexceptional in appearance and mannerisms; in fact, he was as ordinary as his unmemorable name, and it was obvious that he was unaware of this and would not have understood my meaning had I explained it to him. He was simply your normal friend in his late twenties, with dull eyes and short black hair, clothed in a gray coat with a black collar and blue trousers. He was also slightly larger than average. He had the same appearance as a million other men I saw in Manhattan or anywhere else: men who, in the big picture, could be total jerks or wonderful people. But I had no ill will toward him, even though his simple and provincial demeanor stole a remarkable woman from me. Instead, the woman's decision made me feel so sick that I almost passed out on the table.

She continued to speak, prodded by my silence, and now discussed the pointlessness of our relationship, which she claimed had been obvious to her from the minute I talked to her on that stupid train. She then said she was counting on my empathy and apologized for getting me into this hopeless hassle because I appeared like a kind guy whose feelings she hadn't meant to damage. Then she started moving in circles, as though she didn't know if she should continue apologizing or turn her apology into an attack.

I just wanted to hear the man's voice and find anything that would make him valuable, and that was all I wanted then. I realized within two minutes that he couldn't accomplish it by himself. Since taking a seat, he had become less fearful and showed nearly scorn in his eyes as if he thought I was the same kind of milksop he was. I was staring at him, thinking about how I would respond if we had to go at each other bare-faced since I had entirely forgotten about the female. He was heavier than I was, too— at least thirty pounds heavier—with broad bones that gave muscles plenty of room to expand. Unfortunately, his pasty wrists gave the impression that he didn't exercise because he might have enhanced his reputation with just two hours a week at the gym.

It gave me sympathy for him. I asked him how he was feeling, breaking off the female in the middle of another digression. He paused before grudgingly declaring that everything was well. I asked whether he was uncomfortable with the conversation in a sincere, concern-filled tone. He also claimed it was all right. When I inquired whose idea it was to have this confrontation, he responded that it was his girlfriend's, referring to her by name. This was his first multisyllabic statement, but it still denied me an honest look at his character. He stated it didn't matter how they had met when I asked. When I inquired about how I met her, he indicated it was irrelevant.

Any sympathy I had left me at that time. It was intolerable; he was worse than I had imagined. I asked him whether he knew that I had slept with his girlfriend on our first date, that she came three times that night, and that the following morning, she told me she had just had the best sex of her life. I asked him this in a fit of lurid inspiration, hoping to get something respectable out of him. With a barely noticeable wince, he reiterated that it was all insignificant.

Then it dawned on me. I understood why she had selected that man—not just over me, but over every other man in her life—because he was trustworthy. He would forgive her for anything she did if they shared a bed. That is the definition of attractiveness, is it not? That "hard and tumultuous nature" she spoke of was entirely her own; if that man had his way, their relationship would be the most stable. However, she decided it would be too monotonous and instead decided to have a foot in each universe, which left her a little stretched in the middle.

I recalled my approach to her on the train. Having just done what my CEO said was impossible, I felt very good. I always felt like I could do anything, so I brought that attitude into our chat, and when I asked her to meet again, nothing could stop me—no woman could have said no to a man like that. We had a similar first date—me being one of my best selves—and ended up at my flat. She was much more amazing than I had anticipated, and I had no excuse to disappoint her. However, by the next morning, I had become apathetic and had much less energy than she had. She must have called off our second date because, at that point, she would have wanted to ignore the contrast, still feeling euphoric about the evening.

I had felt content that day. It must have raised an alarm that I was as easily as a guy can be with his beloved. My sound was very loud. The fact that the entire spectrum was positive didn't matter because she could envision someone with such a wide range of happy emotions capable of the worst terror. Unlike this guy, her old favorite, whom she could read like a book she had read a dozen times, I was just not as trustworthy. He was also the safest option for any woman, averaging out all potential hazards around a single, stable zero line since there was nothing too awful about him, nothing to jeopardize the comfort of predictability.

After coming to this conclusion, I got up, didn't look at or consider anyone, and left a Jackson on the table for the two glasses of pomegranate juice I had already consumed. I got some fresh air, so I strolled to the World Trade Center. I had to quickly come to terms with the fact that I had lost the lady who had allowed me to move on from Martina and that I would never be able to find another like her again since everything that had happened and everything I was thinking about had culminated in an inevitable conclusion.

Both Hypnosis And Hypnotherapy

In order to cure various psychiatric illnesses, hypnosis is utilized in conjunction with other forms of therapy as a nonstandard or "complementary and alternative" form of treatment.

It produces a heightened level of awareness, sometimes referred to as a trance, through concentrated attention, strong concentration, and guided relaxation. In this state, the person's attention is so narrowly concentrated that they momentarily disregard or block out everything around them.

The person may be able to direct their attention toward particular ideas or tasks with the help of a qualified therapist. It is possible to successfully implement suggestions made while in a hypnotic state into your awake state.

Surprisingly, it is also possible to hypnotize oneself. It is possible to achieve a highly concentrated and attractive frame of mind. It might help you identify and alter undesirable habits and mental patterns and promote calmness.

Similar to this, lucid dreaming enables you to go into a trance in which recommendations could be ingrained in your subconscious.

The primary distinction is that lucid dreaming allows for considerably deeper exploration. There is no state of unconsciousness greater than sleep.

Six Techniques to Promote Lucid Dreaming

Can someone learn how to have lucid dreams?

Simply put, the greatest technique to generate a lucid dream is to become more mind and less body. You can become aware of the space's density by focusing and observing your surroundings.

It means that you have to go from a thinking to a feeling condition.

When you are thinking, most of your mind's activity is devoted to processing and formulating strategies for handling your emotions. In actuality, your ideas are internalized perceptions of the outside environment. Freud knew this as the "reality principle."

However, when you are feeling, you give up trying to think and concentrate instead on the feelings you are experiencing (pain, warmth, comfort, fear, anxiety, and happiness).

VISUAL DIARY

Paying attention to your dreams is the first step towards having a lucid dream. Repetition of the statement "I intend to remember my dreams tonight" could be your action plan.

To ensure that you record everything you recall as soon as you wake up, have a pen and your dream diary close to your bed. It will be a lot easier for you to SEE what your dream patterns are if you put things in writing.

As soon as you can after waking up, do it. Dream recording requires quick thinking and action. The logic of the dream usually escapes you because it doesn't make sense!

WHAT IS A REALITY CHECK, CHAPTER 3?

REALITY CHECKING: WHAT IS IT?

The practice of "reality checking" is rooted in Freud's psychoanalytic theory, which holds that the ego has to distinguish between its internal and exterior worlds. In a psychotherapeutic setting, reality testing is a technique that helps the ego discriminate between fears, beliefs, hopes, and the real world.3.

A straightforward, user-friendly method called "reality checking" can help you become more critical of yourself and develop a habit that will influence your dream behavior.

The process of reality-checking directly addresses the core of lucid dreaming. You need to be able to distinguish between dream and wakefulness in order to have lucid dreams. When you believe, for whatever reason, that you are dreaming, a reality check provides you with a concrete course of action to follow. This will function as a test; if it doesn't pass, it will operate as a catalyst to make your mind acknowledge that you are dreaming.

The reality exam consists of two equally significant sections. The first step is to ask yourself, "Am I dreaming?" critically. The second is to physically carry out the test of your choice to validate or refute your suspicions.

Any action that consistently yields one result while awake and a different result, when you are in a dream state, might be the test. Thankfully, the lucid dreaming community has developed a set of distinct and trustworthy reality tests over years of experimentation:

Breathing Is Impossible: Keeping your mouth shut, squeeze your nose between your thumb and forefinger while you try to inhale. It's a dream if you can make it!

Swapping terms: After reading any written text you can see, look away for a little while and then look back. Did the language change? This also functions with clocks. Was there an abrupt change in time?

The Palm Push: Using your other hand's palm as a guide, gently push two fingers into it. Recall that you want this to occur concurrently with the action.

Examine your hands: In nightmares, hands frequently appear deformed or invisible. Look at your hands and see if each has five fingers. Are your fingers the appropriate size? Is this the correct color?

Examine the mirror: Similar to hands in dreams, distorted reflections are common. Look in the mirror; is everything as it should be?

Light Switch: One peculiarity of dreams is that a light switch is frequently broken. Switching on and off a light is a useful control.

Phantom Hand: Attempting to will your hand to push through a solid object, like a table or wall, is similar to palm pushing.

Phones and Computers: Is the background correct when you turn on your phone or computer? Are those the appropriate programs or apps? These are the specifics that your dream frequently gets wrong.

How to Apply Reality Checks

You can use reality checks to help yourself achieve lucidity in two ways.

Each is founded on a distinct psychological idea:

1. Develop the practice of doing a Reality Check regularly. Doing so will raise the probability that the behavior will be carried over into a dream.

2. Direct your Reality Checks toward particular occurrences; perform a check whenever you see something out of the ordinary or come across something you've already recognized as a dream.

The first approach makes use of a high number of checks to create a large number of transient neural connections. When you dream, your brain is processing the previous day's events. Suppose this includes a lot of reality checks and lucid dreaming thoughts. In that case, there's a greater likelihood that these transient connections will be activated, and the reality check behavior will appear in your dream.

It is possible that the processing will only pick up 2–3% of the controls individually, but it only takes one processed control to provide the trigger for lucidity. You may dramatically improve the probability that at least one control will be triggered during your dream by running 20 or 30 controls during the day.

By focusing on individual events, Reality Checks can be used in a second way that creates stronger neural connections between a certain object or experience and the check-running process through classical conditioning. This enables you to link items that are likely to appear in your dreams with your Reality Checks.

In the long run, this second approach is more efficient, dependable, and effective even though it takes longer to create. You need to have a strong ability to recall dreams and recognize at least a small number of recurrent dreams in order to benefit from this second method.

While reality checks alone can cause lucid dreams, they work best when paired with other methods like LaBerge's Mnemonic Induction of Lucid Dreams, autosuggestion, and intentionality.

Several strategies exist to enhance the Reality Checking method's efficacy; for additional details, refer to the guide on optimizing your reality checks.

Several stories have been published alleging that hypnosis and hypnotherapy are harmful, that they make people into chickens, that people are incapable of waking up, and that unscrupulous hypnotists take advantage of their "prone" clients.

Nonetheless, many believe it has enhanced their lives and enabled them to achieve their objectives. Millions of men and women say that, including IBS, stress, success, phobias, reducing weight, stopping smoking, and other issues.

Too terrified to use this safe and effective healing tool, many individuals are giving up on it.

By responding to these frequently asked concerns concerning hypnotherapy, I hope to allay these fears.

There Are Certain Guidelines You Can Apply To Prepare For Your Own Out-Of-Body Experience.

1. Commence early in the day: As soon as you awaken, begin your journey back to bed. Because of your continued tiredness, you will feel more at ease, and your sense of awareness will not be fully awakened. It is possible to perform astral projection at any time, even if you do not begin first thing in the morning. Just decide what you prefer, and make sure you have the confidence to pursue it.

2. Establish the right atmosphere: You must ensure that you are in a calm and relaxing area. You should do it in your own house to ensure you are completely comfortable.

Try doing astral projection by yourself, if possible, rather than with another person in the room. To avoid being distracted by them wandering around the house or spying on you, try doing it in a different room or while no one else is home.

In order to avoid being distracted by what is happening outside, try drawing the shades as well. Any kind of disturbance or sound can cause you to lose the necessary state of calm.

3. Think positively: Your ability to experience astral projection may be impacted if you're very anxious and exhausted from life's responsibilities. It is important to note that a positive mental attitude increases the likelihood of a positive astral encounter.

4. Once you've selected your room, lie on your back and unwind. Try to block out any outside disturbances. You have to focus on the sensations in your body.

Flex and relax your muscles, beginning with your toes. After your legs are completely relaxed, proceed to your head, focusing on relaxing every muscle in your body.

Make sure your shoulders and chest are relaxed. Simply unwind and inhale deeply, releasing all your air before taking another breath.

Focus on your breathing to prevent your mind from wandering to unrelated thoughts. Don't get too enthusiastic or anxious about the fact that you're trying to achieve astral projection; let the calm seep into your bones.

Some people claim that holding a quartz crystal will help elevate and quicken your body's vibrations while you're getting ready. If you attempt this, be careful to place the crystal on your third eye chakra, which is located directly above your eyebrows.

As soon as you place the crystal on your head, start to calm your mind and feel the vibrations flow through your body. It could be useful for you to visualize a color.

You can hold the crystal in your palm or place it on your chest when you eventually succeed in astral projection. The glass's symbolic purpose is empowering and shielding you from harmful energies.

In order to avoid getting sidetracked by muscle tightness, ensure that your entire body remains relaxed. If you are distracted by anxiety or anything else, it will be more difficult for you to accomplish your astral projection, if it can be accomplished at all.

If necessary, enter a meditation to help you reach the level of calm before attempting to make your astral projection.

Technique of Displaying

It will take some effort to become proficient in this incredibly basic approach, but it can be quite useful for individuals who are more visually oriented. Follow the instructions in the preceding activities to help you into your trance. Start the imagery part of the practice when you are at your deepest level of relaxation.

Focus your concentration on your feet and visualize your spiritual feet inside the physical ones. Gently stretch your active feet to a distance approximately one inch beyond the end of your shoe. After a brief holding period, return your energetic foot to your physical foot. Next, focus on your head, envisioning your active, mental head within your physical one once more. Then stretch your energetic head outward, past the edge of your physical head, by about 1 inch. Reintroduce after a little period of holding.

Lower yourself back to your feet. This time, extend your spiritual feet slightly beyond your physical feet and then retract them. Do the same with your head. Repeatedly extending farther out and pulling back in until you are around two feet beyond your physical body, back and forth between the two. Till the vibrational state is induced, keep rocking in this manner. Once the vibrations are under control, extend mentally till you release your physical body and then move as you like.

You are prepared to leave your physical body now that you have mastered the preparatory steps and attained the vibrating state. Reaching the vibrational state is common, but it is not something you can do independently of your body.

Reacting to what you are going through is the biggest obstacle. Most individuals have read extensively about astral projection and have preconceived notions about what it could feel like. They check for specific checkpoints along the route that signal they are headed in the proper direction.

But doing so maintains your focus on your physical body. The most crucial thing to do when you've attained the vibrating state is to move your awareness outside your body.

You will probably find it very hard to separate, so keep your attention on all bodily sensations to ensure you are moving in the proper direction. You have to ignore all of it and direct your attention elsewhere, away from yourself and all of the feelings you are going through.

The first few times you try to separate, you will find it difficult to focus on all the bodily sensations you are experiencing. This is typical. You will likely need to go through the experience a few times before setting aside your emotions and concentrating on separating.

It is possible to focus your attention outside of your body and make your leave through various separation procedures. You'll need to determine which approach best suits your traits and style.

I'll now go over a few distinct detachment techniques. You can select the one that works best for you once you are comfortable with various approaches.

Chapter 6: Customary methods: customs and antiquated customs.

Is there not a sort of ancient magic that seeps into your blood each time we close our eyes and enter the dream realm? Dreams and visions have a rich history in human history. In the days before smartphones and apps, our predecessors used unique techniques to navigate the dream world. That's why you delved into the world of contemporary tools in Chapter 5, but what if I told you that the most potent methods are the ones we've been using for thousands of years?

Why is it so important to grasp and comprehend these conventional methods? For the straightforward reason that they are the foundation of all that we now know about lucid dreaming. Furthermore, even though science and technology have progressed, these archaic methods retain unrepeatable wisdom.

Have you ever wondered why something that has been practiced for eons and is fundamental to our species has either been forgotten or labeled as "esoteric"? Consider it. Everything needs to be digital, quick, and efficient in the modern world. But isn't it interesting how, despite all our progress, we still go to our past for solutions?

In his 1995 book "Dreamweavers: Traditions of Lucid Dreaming Across Cultures," anthropologist and novelist Timothy Walker reminds us that lucid dreaming practices have been crucial to many cultures. Dream awareness and control have long been considered spiritual and therapeutic powers, a skill valued by Tibetan monks and Siberian shamans alike.

The idea that despite our diverse cultural backgrounds, we are all connected by a common interest in the fantastical realm always makes me grin. Yes, we may have apps and gadgets, but what if the real secret to lucid dreaming lies in practices and methods that our ancestors were already familiar with?

I will leave you with this thought: Don't you think we could have a more profound and real understanding of ourselves and the art of lucid dreaming if we could somehow connect with that ancient knowledge and those rituals performed around campfires under starry skies?

I encourage you to connect with the part of yourself that yearns for wisdom that has been lost and to keep an open mind and heart as you work through this chapter. Even though this voyage might lead us into the past, I can assure you that it will set you up for a future full of more profound and important lucid dreams.

Are you prepared to discover the mysteries of the past and master age-old methods that have been tried and true for many generations? Now, let's go on.

As we move on, you should be aware that every culture has inherited lucid dreaming practices and rituals passed down through the generations. These rituals' richness comes from their capacity to link us to the very fabric of history and tradition, in addition to our minds. I urge you to try it even if you are dubious. You'll be astounded at how much more effective these antiquated techniques can be than contemporary ones.

Consider the Native American "Dream Dance" ceremony. Jacob Midnight's 1988 book "Visions of the Night: Native American Dream Rituals," tells how Indian tribes would get together on new moon evenings to dance, sing, and enter trances. This dance served as a group method for lucid dream induction and a celebration. Through these ceremonies, individuals could reach deeper psychological levels and obtain visions and guidance for the tribe. Can you picture the force of a group ritual directed toward a shared objective?

The Tibetan "Yoga of Sleep" techniques must also be mentioned. Over the ages, Tibetan monks have honed the art of keeping the mind active while the body sleeps. Tenzin Rinpoche claims that this type of yoga is a means of preparing for death and the afterlife and a technique for lucid dreaming. You did read correctly. To comprehend the fleeting nature of existence and prepare for the afterlife, Tibetans hold that developing the skill of lucid dreaming is crucial.

What, then, is the commonality across all these old techniques? It's straightforward: aim. In contrast to modern times, when people pursue lucid dreaming for amusement or curiosity, our forefathers did it to establish a connection with the divine, the meaning of life, and the welfare of their community.

You almost get the impression that while you read this, those old voices are whispering in your ear, urging you to become a part of that ancestors' dreaming community. But how can you apply these age-old methods to your contemporary life if you feel that call? That's what we'll investigate further. So prepare to dive into an ocean of ancient wisdom by taking a deep breath, letting go of your expectations, and diving in.

A tangible link to the dreamers of the past is experienced when delving into the great depths of ancestral wisdom. It's time to apply the knowledge of your ancestors to real-world situations by connecting it to examples.

You're not alone if you've ever pondered, "What on Earth did that mean?" after waking up from a strange dream. For generations, people have been captivated by the idea of interpreting dreams as they try deciphering the symbolic meanings and concealed messages inside their nighttime encounters. In order to help you lucidly dream and obtain insights into your concerns and symbolism, we will discuss dream interpretation and its relationship to lucid dreaming in this part.

Dream interpretation is dissecting the themes, symbols, and feelings that appear in your dreams to learn more about your subconscious. Consider it a type of psychological detective work in which you try to figure out the hidden meanings and themes in your dreams' coded language. Dreams can provide important insights into your emotions, unresolved problems, and even hidden aspirations by serving as a window into your inner brain.

Let's now relate this idea to the intriguing field of lucid dreaming. Being lucid in a dream gives you the extraordinary capacity to deliberately investigate and engage with your dream world. Compared to examining your dreams when you wake up, this conscious investigation provides a more direct and immersive opportunity to go into the realm of dream interpretation in real time.

Imagine that during a lucid dream, you are stuck in a maze and are frantically trying to find a way out. Rather than being scared or overwhelmed, take a moment to ask yourself, "What could this symbolize in my waking life?"

Maybe the maze symbolizes a difficult decision you need to make or a difficult issue at work. Through active engagement with your dream symbols and deliberate exploration of their meanings, you can acquire insightful knowledge that could facilitate the resolution of issues and a deeper comprehension of your feelings.

Let's examine one more illustration. You may come across a recurrent figure in a lucid dream with deep significance. You might interact with this character by posing inquiries and delving into their potential roles in your ideal society. You might learn from this exchange that the character represents a significant person or a particular facet of your personality. You can heal any unresolved issues or emotions associated with that character by gaining this information, ultimately enhancing your personal development and self-awareness.

It's critical to remember that dream interpretation is a very subjective and individualized procedure. One person's interpretation of a symbol may be quite different from yours. Keep an open mind and accept the distinct language of your unconscious mind as you set out on your lucid dreaming journey, and let your dreams lead you on a voyage of self-awareness and personal development.

◆◆◆

Since the beginning, dreams have captured our attention and aroused our curiosity. Many psychological theories have been proposed throughout history to explain why people dream and what our minds might be able to learn from these nocturnal experiences. This section will explore well-known theories and their implications for lucid dreaming, including the Threat Simulation Theory, Jung's Compensation Theory, and Freud's Wish Fulfillment Theory.

1. The Wish Fulfillment Theory of Freud

Dreams are a way of wishing wishes to be fulfilled, according to psychoanalyst Sigmund Freud. Per his theoretical framework, dreams serve as a secure medium for us to subconsciously convey our suppressed aspirations and fancies.

Dreams were a means for Freud to get insight into the depths of our unconscious mind.

Regarding lucid dreaming, Freud's theories can be beneficial. You can explore your deepest desires when you become aware because the limitations of reality do not constrain you. This independence can be enlightening and freeing, enabling you to face suppressed feelings and discover more about yourself.

2. The Compensation Theory of Jung

According to the theory put out by Freud's close friend and Swiss psychiatrist Carl Jung, dreams act as a psychological compensation mechanism. According to Jung, dreams provide us with insights into facets of our personalities that we could be oblivious to or ignore in our waking life, assisting in the balancing of our conscious and unconscious brains.

According to this view, lucid dreamers may find that dreams are an effective means of introspection and personal development. You can uncover concealed facets of your personality and correct any imbalances that might hurt your emotional health by actively participating in the content of your dreams and developing an awareness of them.

3. Theory of Threat Simulation

The Threat Simulation Theory, which Finnish psychologist AnttiRevonsuo developed, suggests that dreams act as a type of practice for hazards and obstacles one may face in the real world. This idea suggests that dreaming developed as a survival mechanism to help us simulate dangerous circumstances safely, improving our ability to anticipate and respond to them.

According to the hypothesis of lucid dreaming, dreams can be an important tool for problem-solving and self-improvement. When lucid, you can consciously confront and overcome barriers in your dreams, developing the courage and fortitude required to meet comparable challenges in the outside world.

In conclusion, different psychological theories about why people dream provide various perspectives on the possible advantages of lucid dreaming. Lucid dreaming offers a potent platform for self-discovery and personal growth, whether you're investigating suppressed urges, revealing secret facets of your personality, or practicing for real-life obstacles.

Remember these theories as you delve deeper into lucid dreaming, and don't hesitate to examine your dreams from various angles. Never forget that your dreams mirror your thoughts and that by talking to them, you can get the keys to a more satisfying, fulfilled existence. Are you prepared to start this fascinating voyage of self-discovery and development, dear reader? In the enigmatic realm of dreams, an exciting journey is ahead.

Lucid Dreams as an Inspirational Source

Inspiration is a challenge that faces everyone. It seems to be subtle, especially for those who ought to be creative, like researchers, exhibiting executives, or craftspeople; this is a fantastic way to get people excited. Lucid dreams provide insight into your deep levels of thought. In a Lucid dream, the things you are unaware you have experienced or remembered are stored away in your intuitive brain, waiting for the first person to access them.

Improved Rest

Having lucid dreams has several health benefits, including that you'll experience better, deeper, and more restful sleep. It's amazing if you have trouble falling asleep because mastering a few essential skills can significantly enhance your sleep quality.

Dreaming lucidly fosters increased consciousness.

That's what being increasingly aware of things is what clarity means. By becoming aware of your dream patterns, you're extending awareness into the realm of imagination. What else is a fantasy made of? This mindfulness is an elevated affectability of the material of your mind. As you become more aware of your subconscious during dreams, you also become more aware of its content during waking hours. Similar attention is seen in these two different states of consciousness. Furthermore, what does not get better with increased mindfulness?

You start to "wake up" and relate to the substance of your psyche instead of always acting out of your thoughts and feelings during the day, which is being non-Lucid to them (you're lost in your contemplations and feelings, much as when you're trapped in a non-Lucid dream). Relating to your sentiments and considerations instead of to them is a brilliant strategy. It can give you great serenity and keep you out of trouble.

Learn about the power of decision-making.

You realize you have a choice while you're experiencing lucid dreams. This type of dream, known as witnessing, allows you to observe the fantasy without changing anything; you watch it like a movie without being engrossed in the story (which would make it non-lucid). Alternatively, you may alter specific aspects of the fantasy, such as creating a better resolution. Whatever the situation, you are honing the decision's intensity. You then utilize that control in your day-to-day activities. Are you becoming angry with your chief yet? It's up to you to decide that. You can change your viewpoint, identity, and ability to wake up and take charge of your life.

finding a lost loved one again

Perhaps the greatest benefit of lucid dreaming is that it allows you to reunite with friends or family members you've sadly lost. In your dream, you can collect and converse with them as if they were real.

You will awaken to beautiful memories of that person as if you had JUST spent time with them. If you never had the chance, it's an amazing way to say goodbye to someone.

To sum up, the more you explore the potential uses for lucid dreaming, the more opportunities present themselves. Try your self-reactions and decisions as much as possible, and watch where the skyline leads you. Not a single Lucid dream is wasted. Dreams and your conscious self-image are linked, enabling you to use this imaginary playground for deep self-reflection and nuggets of wisdom. I adore the possibility that clarity affords me; it allows me to soar like an animal with wings and not be scared to take risks or read challenging material. I may visit anyone and take care of my needs.

Beyond the strangeness of wish fulfillment, it also gives me a direct line of communication with the awareness that lies behind the fantasy and my unaware self, enabling me to release old tensions and feelings of fear and to view myself in a whole new perspective. It's wonderful stuff. Learning to Lucid dream is not easy, like anything worthwhile. In any case, anyone may accomplish anything with perseverance and effort. If you are unfamiliar with this concept, you have already begun to sow the seeds of clarity by reading this article.

The Sleep Paralysis Mystery

Do you frequently wake up in the middle of the night feeling as though you are trapped in a vise? Have you ever been frozen and stuck in the middle of sleep in your bedroom with unexplained sensations of a mysterious presence?

A lot of people have reported experiencing the enigmatic phenomena known as sleep paralysis throughout history. There is a stage between wakefulness and sleep where the body is virtually immobile and cannot move or communicate. We call this condition "sleep paralysis." While some people think a supernatural force produces it, others think neurological or psychological problems can cause it. One thing is certain, regardless of the cause: sleep paralysis may simultaneously be interesting and terrifying!

This chapter will examine the enigma surrounding sleep paralysis and explain why some people experience it. We will also investigate the various theories on its causes and how to prevent it. Now, let's get started! Have you ever had paralysis from sleep? What potential causes do you believe it may have? Is it possible for us to completely avoid it? Let's investigate as a group!

Sleep Paralysis: What Is It?

Since ancient times, a large number of people have reported experiencing sleep paralysis globally. When the body teeters between the verge of wakefulness and sleep, it can cause paralysis, rendering you unable to move or speak. Chinese medical texts have recorded this event since the 4th century, but similar accounts may be found in many civilizations worldwide.

It is estimated that 8% of people globally suffer from sleep paralysis. A recent National Sleep Foundation poll verified this is the case. Circumstances, including genetics, disturbed REM cycles, and mental health conditions like PTSD or depression.

What Takes Place During Sleep Paralysis?

Sleep paralysis is not exclusive to any particular demographic. Still, some people might be more vulnerable than others. Many are more likely to suffer from sleep deprivation, narcolepsy, and mental health conditions like anxiety and depression. Stress levels, circadian rhythms, and alcohol or drug use can all be factors in its incidence. It's interesting to note that teens and young adults exhibit more cases because of their different hormone levels and sleep cycle transitions. Don't worry; we'll look into what causes it so you can learn more about how to deal with it.

Scenes

The purpose of landscapes is to give you a broader perspective of what you are experiencing. It seems your brain is telling you to enlarge your view and see the wider picture. Since a landscape can only be observed from a distance, analyzing dreams that feature landscapes from a higher viewpoint opens up a whole new avenue of interpretation. It might highlight areas requiring attention, such as your family, work, or even sincerely held beliefs. Observing the many kinds of landscapes in your dream will help you understand how wide a scope the dream covers.

A barren terrain could suggest that you have a certain amount of baroness. Let's imagine you have a dream in which the middle of a desert serves as your office. This can indicate to you that your work is not rewarding where you are at. An alternative perspective on the same circumstance is that you should work harder at your work. Dryness suggests that nourishment is required. You can tell when a desert scene emerges that something is absent. The specifics of your activities in the desert or the events that are taking place will reveal the areas of deficiency. For instance, if you dream of family members in the desert, something is missing from your family life or relationship.

The wetland or woodland landscape is the antithesis of the desert landscape. This suggests that there is plenty. Your subconscious informs you that your chosen course will pay off when you view a landscape with wetlands. If a marsh setting is the background of your dream, you might assume that success is imminent. Abundance is not just financial; it can permeate many aspects of your life. It might be an abundance of time if you have a hard career or an abundance of love from a spouse or friend.

Mountains are another type of terrain that frequently shows up in dream sequences. Mountains symbolize obstacles. Being at the mountain's peak signifies that you have conquered a challenge in your life; conversely, being in the valley indicates that you still have challenges ahead of you. Additional indicators of your challenges are the quantity of mountains and the climate. Furthermore, the size of the mountains is important. Massive mountains can indicate that you need assistance because the challenge is too great for you to handle alone, but many lesser mountains indicate a difficult journey ahead. While pleasant weather or rain suggests that you have support, cold weather suggests that you could have to confront challenges alone. Mountains can also stand for enlightenment or fresh perspectives. In biblical tradition, Moses is said to have received the Israelite law atop a mountain. Since mountains are land near the sky, reaching their summit can symbolize learning more advanced knowledge.

A coastline symbolizes balance, dualism, or the collision of opposing forces, making it an intriguing environment to see in a dream. The land joins the sea along the shoreline. The river symbolizes your spiritual or emotional life, while the land represents your material or bodily existence, including your assets and finances. In contrast, if the shore is wide and the water is far away, you are not meeting your emotional or spiritual requirements. If the water is destroying the land, it indicates that you need to focus more on your material reality.

Residences, Structures, and Construction Sites

Buildings, homes, cityscapes, and construction sites are all part of the physical world. Man-made structures stand for ambition, riches, and status. Since any construction must be erected, your dream demonstrates your work. This could indicate that you need to work even harder, or it could be a request to increase your effort. The state of the home, structure, or construction indicates the status of your current material reality, just like the other dreamscapes that have been covered previously. Moreover, the kind of building indicates which aspect of your life you are dreaming about repackaging.

Still-in-progress construction sites: This is a fresh, substantial project you are engaged in. This new endeavor could be a business you intend to launch or a new job you have started. An investment you've made can also be compared to a construction site. A crumbling construction site could indicate that you are about to give up on a project or that you should leave now as it will not work. A disorganized building site indicates that your new business is unsure or insecure and that you need to take steps to establish more structure.

It's preferable to continue down your current path if you have an orderly, efficient, and clean building site.

A home addresses more localized issues. Because your home is man-made and you live there, dreams involving houses often highlight material issues that are relevant to you. If you picture a neighborhood full of houses, your dream reflects the issues in your town. This community need only be one you are a part of; it need not be where you now reside. For instance, you might be a member of the fashion community if you are passionate about clothing. If you live in a house, especially if there is just one, this is a closer connection than with your family or life. While spotless homes demonstrate that you are doing well, broken or dirty homes indicate that something has to change or be corrected. Empty or incomplete dwellings are signs that you still have work to do.

A whole cityscape addresses your aspirations. In a larger sense, this aligns with your aspirations and aims. Cities are economic centers and the places where money is made. Consequently, your professional route is closely related to cityscapes' aspirations. A brightly illuminated city indicates a more optimistic outlook on your current professional direction, while a gloomy city suggests that you are somewhat unsure about it. Cities in disrepair indicate a lack of desire for your job. A city under construction is a symbol of your growth and the development of your professional goals. A bustling city is a sign that your vision is taking off. If the city is chaotic, though, that can be a sign that you must make some changes because your vision is in danger.

What is Lucid Dreaming? – Chapter 1.

It's possible that when you started reading this book, you believed lucid dreaming was a strange and wonderful technique. Perhaps you believe that lucid dreams are exclusive to witches or people who have undergone many hours of therapy. In actuality, anyone with the right skills can have lucid dreams. After reading this book through to the end, you will be an expert and well on your way to experiencing your first lucid dream. However, it's crucial to comprehend what one is before understanding how to have one. Establishing a solid understanding base is necessary before applying it in real-world situations.

Researchers and scientists are discovering more and more about lucid dreaming every day. They are watching people who practice lucid dreaming and conducting ground-breaking research. However, one such practitioner can attest that it doesn't require a genius. All it takes to lucid dream is awareness of your subconscious. But if you don't first explore your dreams and learn what your subconscious mind often attempts to teach you, you won't be able to tune into that area of your brain. To accomplish this, break down a dream's essence first, then proceed.

Dreams: What Are They?

A dream is an aspiration from the heart. I apologize; that is Cinderella. There are many songs, books, and movies about dreaming, so get accustomed to the corny quotes. For what reason is that the case? Because dreaming has always interested us. It makes some sense, sort of. We can launch spacecraft into orbit and explore the ocean's depths, but we cannot put a study team inside the human mind now. Recounting dreams carries a significant inaccuracy because they occur when we are asleep. Many people wake up from their dreams unable to recall every detail, making it impossible for them to explain what happened and why. To put it briefly, there is an air of mystery around dreams. Scientifically speaking, they are simply the results of your synapses firing during sleep. Later on, we'll discuss the many sleep cycles. For now, just remember that your brain passes through several stages of sleep during the night and that your subconscious tends to get wild during the most peaceful part of the sleep cycle.

Strangely, while your body is physically resting, your mind is still at work. Your subconscious thoughts come to life in your dreams. You see, your mind has two layers: the conscious and the subconscious. All of your day-to-day thoughts are contained in your conscious mind. Every day (well, most days), you intentionally roll out of bed and get ready for work. When you get to work, your mind is overrun by ideas and tasks you must process or ignore. After work, you deliberate on what to dress, eat, and do with your free time. The subconscious mind is more intricate. Consider the subconscious mind as everything underneath the iceberg's surface and the conscious mind as its tip. Your whole thought and belief system, dating back to your earliest childhood memories, is in your subconscious. It's the place where your most painful memories and awkward thoughts reside. It even keeps track of the thoughts you consciously choose to ignore. Our whole self is kept safe and well in our subconscious's incredible vault. If you ignore the lower portion of the iceberg, your entire existence could sink like the Titanic.

The subconscious mind has a door that is cracked open while we sleep. Things that you usually don't think about during the day come to light. Dreams can take many forms, such as playing in the park or unexpectedly finding yourself in the middle of an important business presentation. They can also be quite strange—like when you're playing in the park and suddenly realize that you're a rabbit. Everyone seated at the table in the presentation meeting you mentioned earlier is an old crush you haven't thought much about in years. Better yet, they're all laughing at you while you're nude. Like a great novel or an amusement park, dreams can be enjoyable, but they can also be stressful. I once dreamed that a lion chased me on an expressway, but I wasn't in a car. I was walking on the freeway for some reason, which added to the horrific experience. The lion would not stop chasing me, even when I dove between oncoming automobiles to escape him. When I woke up, my heart was racing.

Our minds select the dreams they do for a variety of reasons. There is occasionally a correlation between what we eat and the vividness of our dreams. Many claim that after eating a spicy meal, they experience especially vivid nightmares. Our subconscious will occasionally become activated by the stress we experience regularly, compelling us to revisit some of the more upsetting parts of our day. Our amount of conscious tension can occasionally determine our subconscious nightmares. Repressed trauma can occasionally materialize in dreams, reminding us of things we make a great effort to forget.

Overall, dreams might be directed or arbitrary. They may originate from recollections from the past or present and aspirations for the future. They can be comprehended and interpreted in certain situations, while they have no meaning at other times. It is easy to interpret dreams too literally, but it is also possible to miss clues in dreams and misinterpret what your subconscious is attempting to convey. If you can just take charge of your thoughts and access your subconscious, you can learn more about what is happening there. Your dreams might have the universe's fundamental code or the words to Barney's "I Love You."

Now that you know the fundamentals of dreams, let's discuss how trying to control them is known as lucid dreaming. *Lucid dreaming* is a taught talent that takes patience and practice to master. Others characterize it as being aware while having a dream (Nunez, 2019). However, that description is a little deceptive. It is still your physical unconsciousness that prevents you from dreaming. Your mind, however, awakens and becomes capable of processing the surrounding data. If you've watched the film Inception, you've seen an extreme case of lucid dreaming. Not only is the dreamer conscious in that film, but other people can infiltrate a dream and exert mental control over the dreamer.

Do not be alarmed because there is currently no technology that can breach a dream. You can still "wake up" in your dream and explore a little. You could convince yourself that this isn't real. This tactic is particularly useful for nightmares and dreams involving hot food. I'm only dreaming. You can relax and take charge of the dream's events. Your subconscious usually writes your dreams, but your conscious mind takes charge when you have lucid dreams.

The Lucid Visions

The Definition of Lucid Dreaming
What, then, is a lucid dream? To put it quite simply, it's the dream that you have a conscious influence over. Frederik Willem van Eden was the first to use this phrase. In 1913, the year Freud published The Interpretation of Dreams, he used this word in his paper A Study of Dreams. Permit me to introduce this chapter with a few definitions from well-known lucid dreaming authors.

In his book Remote Viewing Secrets, Joseph McMoneagle cited Stephen LaBerge, Ph.D., a Stanford University Sleep Research Center specialist, who explained that lucid dreaming is simply "being awake in your dreams." This is not the same as daydreaming or "dreaming while you are awake." We do not sleep when we are daydreaming. On the other hand, dreaming awake implies that we are awake during sleep. We each have two selves: the sleeping half and the awake part. We also recognize that we are dreaming. This could be one of

81

the explanations for why lucid dreaming is occasionally called conscious dreaming.

In her book The Art of Lucid Dreaming: The Pursuit of Conscious Dream, Rebecca Turner's ability to deliberately monitor and/or influence your dreams is known as controlling lucid dreaming. To be able to manage the dream, one must be awake or conscious. Consequently, "lucid dreaming" and "dream control" are not new.

Four specialists from different fields (Daniel et al.) described a lucid dream as one in which the dreamer is aware that they are dreaming, as stated in an original scientific paper published by Front Psychology Journal. This term, however, was taken with a little wording change from LaBerge's book.

I want to conclude by sharing with you the definition provided by Professor BeritBroogard, D.M.Sc., Ph.D. She described lucid dreaming (in Psychology Today) as an opportunity to experiment with the remarkable skills hidden in underutilized brain regions.

According to the definitions found on these pages, lucid dreaming is essentially just a dream with two extra characteristics: it is somewhat controllable and vivid. And if that's the case, what makes lucid dreaming unique? Experts did not even inform us that lucid dreaming holds greater significance than regular dreaming. It is argued that whereas lucid dreaming lacks a purpose or meaning, ordinary dreaming does. For this reason, Broogard stated that it's an opportunity to have fun. It's only a play. Well, don't let my cheap temptation worry you. Understanding lucid dreams is unnecessary, but as Broogard noted, it's one method to unlock the incredible potential hidden in underutilized brain regions. I believe that exceptional powers are hidden in the subconscious mind, as Boogard intended to imply that being human is super and that you can dream of being Superman. Understanding the power of the subconscious mind is possible through lucid dreaming.

The Purposes of Dream Interpretations

The claim that "lucid dreaming is not more important than ordinary dreaming" has some light in it. "The function" means that lucid dreaming is not entirely pointless. Its features can answer many people's questions concerning their need for this type of dreaming. In order to save you time, I'll keep it brief.

Mental Retraining

Not at all! Not that you can take over people's thoughts, mind you. This is what I mean. Your ability to regulate your mind will increase as you practice lucid dreaming.

You will discover later on that lucid dreaming practice necessitates mental control. It is almost hard to regulate the mind. It is quite difficult. The phrase "mind control" refers to releasing oneself from mental dominance.

We tend to hop from one thought to the next when we control our minds or are recognized as minds. Being mindful during this condition is incredibly challenging, even though attention is essential to having effective lucid dreams. How can you be aware that you are dreaming if you are not mindful? That's the main idea. You must use mindfulness when training yourself to acquire this talent. Mindfulness is necessary for all spiritual and psychic activities.

Self-awareness is encouraged by mindfulness, which has countless positive effects on day-to-day living. Being aware of oneself is crucial not only when dreaming but also when one is awake. This is the first use of lucid dreaming that gives you the biggest advantages.

Self-Reflection

No doubt. You go into the infinite depths of your inner self through lucid dreaming. Lucid dreaming must be the process of self-exploration since dreams essentially express our unconscious desires or wishes hidden deep within our unconsciousness, whether we are aware of them or not.

Although everyone can lucid dream, each person is different. The experiences you have during lucid dreaming are distinct and cannot be compared to those of others. While experiencing an out-of-body experience can be similar from person to person, the experience itself cannot be replicated.

We own this planet. We exchange items. But you own your subconscious mind. You live in this world. Your database, which governs 95% of your life, is located there. Investigating this "world" entails investigating oneself. Having lucid dreams helps you better comprehend who you are rather than the lucid dreaming.

An elevated consciousness

A higher awareness can be attained by gaining new insights into dimensions beyond this physical one.

You will become increasingly conscious of the existence of dimensions other than the physical one if you experience lucid dreams. Your subconscious is a realm, a "mental warehouse" where you store and/or constrain your powers. We live like machines. We continue to follow our everyday routines and familiar lives until we finally become lost. Lack of self-awareness is one of the upper-class aspects of living like a robot. We become more aware of our existence when we raise our level of self-awareness.

As a result, there is a great chance that our lives will improve. We can reclaim control over our lives, including our desires, actions, and so on. Furthermore, it's no secret that becoming more conscious of oneself makes one wiser. "Wiser" refers to the ability to avoid making poor choices.

Getting Rid of the Limiting Ideas

Dream killers are limiting ideas. They destroy your creativity, drive, and will to live a better life. Beliefs that limit your potential include those that you think you can't, that you're unfortunate, that you're unimportant, that you're not special, that you think it's impossible (whatever it is), and so forth.

These are the ideas that keep you from realizing all of your life's potential. They prevent you from reaching greater and bigger heights. Overcoming these assumptions when you are awake is not a simple task. Overcoming them in lucid dreaming is simpler.

It has been explained that lucid dreaming is somewhat under your control. Lucid dreaming entails managing the neurological process in your brain since lucid (or regular) dreaming is a neurological process. Take a look. Your brain's synapses are altered when you learn a new language. New synaptic lines are formed whenever you acquire new information. Your brain's synaptic pathways change as a result of your new habits. Accordingly, whatever tiny modification you make while in a lucid dream will nevertheless occur.

Neurologically, the fixed mindset or limiting ideas is a synaptic pattern. By lucid dreaming, you can overcome your limiting beliefs and shift your perspective.

Are you familiar with hypnosis in any way? You probably do. A customer receiving hypnotherapy was assisted in accessing his subconscious. The hypnotist assisted him in seeing himself swimming. This was a phobia for the customer. The client found swimming difficult even in the hypnotic condition or with a strong imagination. In the end, he succeeded. This phobia's agony comes to an end. Though it delivers a shift in perspective, hypnotic imagination is less lucid than lucid dreaming. Dreaming of lucidity is far superior to that.

Getting to the Solution

You were dilemmatic once. You informed your pal that you require an update from her. She said, "Ask yourself." How is that possible?

Spiritualists claim that each of us contains the real Guru. Experience is the true teacher, according to modern culture. It's known as the higher self in the new age. Regardless of the word you prefer, this one must be met. It's not talking about your heart. It alludes to the true you—the more mature, self-aware, and reflective version of yourself.

According to certain antiquated beliefs in East Indonesia, encountering oneself in a dream portends impending death. It's thought that your higher self is alerting you of the impending departure from this body. It arrives to bid you farewell. Yes, it is rather perplexing, isn't it? It signifies the end of your relationship with your egos (body, intellect, and heart).

You can meet "this person" in lucid dreaming to find the solution to an issue. The inquiry must concern your life. For instance, there may be a time in your life (like a marriage) when you are unsure about what to do. You might connect with your higher self or the inner Guru to make that decision. It might seem great occasionally, but it might also sometimes just look like you in the mirror.

Healthy sleeping practices

After mastering good sleep hygiene, concentrate on developing more restful sleeping practices. One of the most important things in our lives is sleep. We tend to overlook that. In addition to helping you mentally and physically prepare for lucid dreaming, maintaining sound sleeping habits offers many other advantages. However, let us continue to concentrate on the steps you must take to form sound sleeping habits (Yuschak, 2006; Holzinger et al., 2006; Suni, 2009; Summer, 2022).

Make time for sleep: A restful night's sleep is essential to one's health and well-being. Lack of sleep impairs emotions, mental function, and even physical health. Additionally, since you need a clear, active mind to recognize that you are dreaming, it may make lucid dreaming more challenging.

A nightly schedule: Your evening routine ought to be peaceful and restful. To establish a calm environment for sleeping.

Regularly practice meditation: Stress management greatly benefits from meditation. Regular mindfulness meditation.

Use visualization methods: You may train your mind to have lucid dreams using visualization techniques. You can learn to recognize when you are dreaming and when you are not by practicing self-awareness and envisioning what you hope to experience in a lucid dream.

Sleep aids: Essential oils and herbal teas can assist in promoting better sleep by calming the mind. They must, however, be used cautiously and under a healthcare provider's supervision.

Avoid stimulants: They can interfere with sleep and make it harder to maintain lucid dreams. Examples of stimulants include caffeine and smoking. Three hours should pass before going to bed, if possible.

Practice remembering dreams: The ability to recollect one's dreams after waking up is known as dream recall. This skill is essential for lucid dreaming since it makes it possible for you to become increasingly aware of your dream state. To improve dream recollection, keep a dream journal.

You are halfway done with lucid dream preparation if you have established your sleep schedule and finally gained control over your sleeping patterns.

Let's take a closer look at some other items that will aid in better preparing your experience.

Comparing LsdWith Other Recreational Substances

LSD is a very special kind of recreational drug. It has both psychedelic and hallucinogenic properties. The various features and elements that distinguish LSD from other recreational drugs are numerous.

Cannabis vs. LSD

Both marijuana and ergot LSD are natural substances. Both substances can open the mind, alter consciousness, and produce hallucinations. The similarities between these two medications stop there, though.

The high from marijuana differs greatly from the high from LSD. Marijuana is more focused on the body, whereas LSD is more cerebral. Marijuana is a sedative, and LSD is a stimulant. LSD has far more potent mental effects than marijuana, even at relatively low dosages. While under the influence of marijuana, the ordinary user may still function in public; nevertheless, for certain individuals, LSD can completely impair their capacity to function.

Ecstasy vs. LSD

It is possible to purchase ecstasy and LSD as pills. Sometimes, the effects of both drugs are combined by dipping ecstasy into a solution of LSD. Although ecstasy isn't considered a hallucinogen, its formulation may include some hallucinogenic elements in it. Both substances are illegal worldwide, have been used in psychological warfare trials, and lower inhibition. They also produce jaw tightness, fluid loss, and light sensitivity.

Ecstasy and LSD are two distinct substances with quite different effects. Ecstasy is a bodily high, whereas LSD is more of a mental high. LSD does not play on hormones the way ecstasy does. While the aftereffects of ecstasy are unpleasant, those of LSD tend to be more uplifting.

PCP vs. LSD

PCP and LSD are very different from one another. That is all there is to it: they are both recreational drugs. PCP is a dissociative anesthetic, whereas LSD is a psychedelic drug. While PCP induces relaxation and drowsiness, LSD increases alertness and induces insomnia. PCP increases a user's ego, whereas LSD reduces their sense of self. While LSD produces vivid images and synesthesia, PCP causes the user to lose mental awareness of their body.

Psychedelic vs. LSD fungi

"Shrooms" and LSD are two substances that provide psychedelic effects. Both of them are tryptamine compounds that are generated from fungus. Bad trips can also result from both psychedelics.

The experience with mushrooms differs greatly from the experience with LSD. The mushroom high is more focused on nature, but the LSD high is brighter and more colorful. While the effects of mushrooms only endure for six hours, those of LSD last for about twelve.

Anxiety levels induced by LSD are lower than those of mushrooms. Compared to mushrooms, LSD produces a less incapacitating high. LSD users can be more social butterflies than mushroom users, typically more couch potatoes. While mushrooms need a higher amount to have the same effect, LSD merely needs a smaller dose to cause hallucinations.

Cocaine vs. LSD

Cocaine and LSD are two common options for recreational use. Both drugs are stimulants that might cause suicidal thoughts and make users talkative and gregarious. On the other hand, LSD is less expensive than cocaine. Additionally, the LSD high lasts far longer than the cocaine high. LSD is also a lot safer than cocaine. An overdose of cocaine is likely to be fatal, while an overdose of LSD is almost impossible to survive. While cocaine is addictive, LSD is not. While cocaine can harm the nose and heart, LSD does not always cause organ damage.

Heroin vs. LSD

Not only do near-death experiences (NDEs) frequently involve an out-of-body experience, but they can also revert to lucid dreams, as retired physicist John Wren-Lewis experienced.

One evening, he started to worry that the wine he had consumed would interfere with the mystical awareness that had arisen after his near-death experience. That evening, he became lucid in a dream: "I understood this to be a dream where my spectral invisibility represented my post-NDE state, and the dream characters who saw me were the people who realized in the real world that I was living in heaven here on earth, dead to 'this world.'" Wren-Lewis understood that the purpose of this dream was to investigate his apprehension regarding the impact of the wine on his recently awakened consciousness. He realized that the main danger to his mystical consciousness, as he lay in bed in his Australian flat, had little to do with alcohol per se; rather, it was about getting sucked into an internal debate about alcohol. I entered the dream area and walked right through the wall to celebrate this milestone in terms of dreams. My dream was filled with spiritual consciousness as I exited the street beside Sydney

Harbor. This was not a novel experience but a realization of what had been there all along. This is the same feeling I get when returning to the mystical consciousness in my waking life. I was carried over the lake by a wind that I recognized as God's breath on the first morning of creation, and I passed out from the sheer beauty of it all. I woke up in bed with tears of gratitude in my eyes. In this case, Wren-Lewis reinforced the mystical (perhaps "pure") awareness resulting from a near-death experience via a lucid dream.

Some aspects of lucid dreaming, OBEs, and NDEs may also be present in UFO "experiences." Many of these events may be dreams that have been misconstrued. During such an encounter, the person feels as though aliens have kidnapped, studied, and perhaps experimented on him or her. Frequently, the victim of abduction suppresses memories of the typically traumatic and agonizing experience, revealing information only when hypnotized. Ring states, "At the phenomenological level, NDEs and UFO [experiences] are quite dissimilar, but it is in their 'deep structure,' as it were, rather than in their surface contextual manifestations that important commonalities can be discerned." In other instances, however, those blocked memories might be forgotten dreams.

For example, veteran lucid dreamer Alan Worsley reveals that he has occasionally found himself at the mercy of aliens when he causes lucid dreaming by lying still on his back for as long as two hours or longer. I don't believe in "unnecessary entities" or superstition, but maybe the word "dream" is a bit too neutral to describe the intense realism of these experiences, he says.

For example, it can be quite challenging to remain motionless if one "dreams"—as I have—of being examined by robots in the dark, operated upon by tiny beings whose competence and good intentions may be questioned, or mistreated in other ways by life-forms unknown to terrestrial biology. I have discovered that this unusual awareness generally passes quickly if I am not motionless. As a means of escape, that can be quite helpful, but when it takes two hours or longer to complete each try, and the success rate is low, it can be frustrating to lose it. I consider myself to be at least a reasonably intrepid investigator. However, I must confess that, although I was convinced intellectually that what was occurring was simply an internally created vision, I have recoiled several times during these episodes... I suspect that a lot of reports of "UFO abductions" and out-of-body experiences are instances of the same type of phenomena.

Mark, a prosperous North Carolina businessman, provides an amazing illustration of the connection between OBEs, NDEs, UFO experiences, and lucid dreams. Mark has had OBEs whenever he has wanted them since he was a young child. They are peaceful and not menacing, he clarifies. Additionally, he frequently becomes lucid after one and a half hours of sleep and stays that way for the rest of the night. He describes feeling completely aware but at ease and always in perfect control of the activity. He and his mother experienced their first abduction by UFOs when they were teenagers, and aliens took them to a spaceship for examination. Mark told himself over and over again that he was dreaming during that whole encounter. He also frequently sleepwalks, even though he woke up with mud on his feet because the aliens had led them through a muddy area. Mark has had a lifetime of amazing encounters with consciousness, enabling him to easily switch between imaginal states.

It is vital to emphasize that all of these experiences—OBE, NDE, lucid dream, and UFO abduction—have a strongly felt realism. And maybe because of the intensity of sensation, the uninformed viewer frequently concludes that the experience is "real," much like commuting to work or putting the kids to bed is "real." We both acknowledge that alternative explanations might exist, even though we contend that these experiences do not reflect "objective" reality. These encounters put our ideas of what is "real" to the test. To write these experiences off as existing "outside" of generally acknowledged reality would be a mistake. Such experiences, particularly lucid dreaming, challenge our understanding of what it means to be "awake" and what reality is, as we demonstrate in other sections of this book.

Chapter: When not to use an astral projection

There is no reason why Astral Projection shouldn't be safe if it is done in a secure setting and with all the required safety precautions. Remember that Astral Projection is only a mental means of transportation, not a physical one. Your body won't be more dangerous than it is if you manage to have any out-of-body experiences.

Many falsehoods and stories are circulating regarding the dangers of Astral Projection.

Is it possible for your body and consciousness to become permanently apart?

Is it possible to pass away while experiencing an out-of-body state?

When astral projecting, are you susceptible to possession?

Can beings harm you on the astral planes?

These are only a few of the frequently encountered anxieties; I'll do my best to address a few of them and ease your concerns.

You can be confident that you cannot live apart from your body. Put an end to your concerns if you think your awareness will somehow stray from your physical body.

Your physical body and consciousness are inextricably linked by what some refer to as a "Silver Cord." That invisible link ensures that you will never entirely lose your path, even if you go a vast distance and notice a tiny delay in returning to your body. Even if it takes some time, you will always find your way back to your physical self.

More importantly, for those unfamiliar with astral travel, the matter of death might raise serious concerns. Your body is not moving when experiencing an out-of-body experience; your consciousness is moving. This implies that your body is still as dangerous as it is at any other moment, so as long as you practice Astral Projection in a safe and secure environment, you should be okay. On the other hand, you will undoubtedly be in danger if you choose to use Astral Projection someplace risky, like the side of a busy road!

You're most likely worried about the chance that your awareness will pass away while it's still apart from your body. The problem with this is that if anyone has ever experienced this in the past, they are no longer with us to share their story! Therefore, we cannot determine with certainty whether or not your awareness can pass away when astral projecting.

That being said, it's highly unlikely that your mind could pass away and cause your body to pass away, given what we know about Astral Projection, how entities can interact with your consciousness, and the connection between your consciousness and your physical body.

To be clear, this is quite unlikely. It's so unlikely that I don't think it's worth worrying about. That said, even if it does happen, you won't ever find out!

We do have some knowledge of how other entities in the astral realms may interact with you, as I indicated before. This brings me to our next common concern, which is being possessed.

In other words, when you are in the Astral Projection state, you are not susceptible to possession. While some entities may feel a little off, they must attach themselves to something tangible to become possessed.

Remember that when you are experiencing an out-of-body experience, your mind is actually exploring the astral planes rather than anything physical; in other words, your consciousness is out of your body. This implies that even if an entity tried to take possession of you, it couldn't succeed as it wouldn't have your actual body to cling to.

Because of this, Astral Projection differs greatly from other practices like using Ouija boards. Using an Ouija board, you can invite other beings to visit your mind and body, which are still connected. In such a scenario, it would be simple for them to attach themselves to your physical body, which isn't feasible with Astral Projection. You cannot allow negative creatures to enter your physical body during out-of-body experiences.

In the same manner, nothing at all can hurt your body. This is because they can only enter your mind, not your physical body.

Horror tales of extraterrestrials or other beings probing or attacking people are certainly familiar to you, but they are merely stories. No force may physically damage your body in any way.

Later in the book, we shall go over the subject of other entities on the astral worlds again.

Even if your actual body may be secure, some out-of-body experiences can undoubtedly feel unreal. The procedure itself can be extremely mentally taxing, and some of the things you will witness will be, to put it mildly, eye-opening. Because of this, I advise against using Astral Projection if you suffer from any kind of underlying psychological disorder.

Astral projection is an incredible experience, but remember that the mind is delicate. There's no reason to take the chance of adding further imbalances to your already unstable consciousness.

Dreams With Lucidity

In every aspect, lucid dreaming is the most thrilling type of dreaming. This dreaming is described as a situation in which the dreamer exercises free will and control over the dream after realizing they are dreaming.

The term "lucidity" refers to the awareness that arises when you dream at night and realize that you are truly resting in bed while simultaneously exploring a subconscious dream world.

For example, this condition is ideal because it has a therapeutic effect and can turn any nightmare into a pleasant experience. Another form of therapeutic dreaming is lucidity. Additionally, it boosts self-esteem while giving ample room to practice skills that are challenging in daily life. Even while many individuals often sneak with years of experience because they think they once made the incorrect decision, a situation that they have always desired to handle, like a rendezvous with their favorite actor or a coveted but never obtained teenage swarm, can be pretty liberating and very healing.

Since no one is hurt, allowing its shoots complete freedom is also possible. You can compare a lucid dream to a computer game where you can go and do everything you want, but with far better graphics and a more straightforward experience!

In lucid dreams, the sensation of reality is as strong and genuine as in the awake state. You can teach yourself to overcome your small instability since you must wake up when you accomplish your dream. There have been over a hundred reports of lucid dreams, including many that I have already had:

The entire scene became immediately apparent when I understood I was dreaming—it was like being on the road in my life! Everything that I could reach and experience as though it were genuine. As I drove by, I got a kick out of a bush with amazing, mysterious leaves that were so juicy and vivid green that they tickled my palms. It was an amazing event that gave me a profound sense of balance and happiness, as though I had found a long-lost planet that I had found again.

The typical dream, often called a dull dream, is just a memory that remains in the memory upon awakening in the morning. In contrast, lucid dreaming is an act of verification; in other words, the dream becomes an immediate present instead of ending as a mere memory in the morning.

It is possible to feel the deepest desires in addition to being able to direct and control every feasible action. In addition, this can be used therapeutically to assist individuals in overcoming phobias, disappointments, unfulfilled desires, or frustrations. It would be possible for any desired companion to actively participate in the dream. Here, the choices are quite endless.

As is common, I felt like I was flying during the next encounter. Flying through the sky or a landscape feels incredibly freeing and lovely. The therapeutic demand is also evident and adds flavor to daily existence: I ran away from some men who were most likely going to find me, but then I became conscious and realized what was going on. I halted there and turned to face my attackers. They felt that I was determined, and they were afraid to hurt me anymore. The throng gradually dispersed as they cast nearly innocent glances at the nearby area or the ground. Following that, I decided to try my hand at flying. I launched into a stunning blue sky and relished the vista and the breeze.

Alternatively, click this:

I was standing in a bedroom I didn't know existed, facing a huge mirror, when I suddenly realized I was dreaming. My surroundings instantly became completely clear, allowing me to see every detail. He was fluffy and felt real as I knelt to touch the carpet. I could even make out tiny structures and filaments. I then sat once more and moved my eyes around, not focusing or fixing anything to prolong and strengthen this dream. Once I was sufficiently rigid, I strolled through the bedroom. I could not remember anything, but it seemed strangely familiar.

Or this one: I had a lucid dream again and realized with amazing clarity that I was experiencing a strong curiosity and the urge to fly or simply enjoy myself at that same moment.

I realized I was in a huge hotel lobby as I turned to look around. To my right, I noticed a friend getting closer to me. She grinned and said hello to me. I told her we were dreaming and could do anything we wanted when she stood beside me. She gave me a bewildered expression. With my right hand, I extended my reach and produced a ball. She was in awe. After that, we laughed and threw caution to the ball in this enormous hotel hall. There was much to shatter.

The possibilities are endless here, and upon returning from such experiences and reawakening in the physical body, they invariably give rise to truly tangible and intense energies. I've had occasions when I've been able to sustain my energy for a week or two.

Events in daily life that are most fascinating and thrilling are made possible by such psychic forces. Concentrating is enhanced, perception is sharper and more sustained, and attention is focused. Only the dreamer himself may experience and benefit from these vast advantages.

For me, spontaneous lucidity occurred frequently. When you've had some training in lucid dreams—many people have already learned about it—you can enter this condition on your own, seemingly for no obvious reason, or by doing the current exercise that allows you to return to the dream after you wake up.

While standing in the kitchen, a buddy I was visiting called from across the room. Their contradicting statement—which I can't recall—led me to believe I was dreaming. Suddenly, everything around me made sense.

I examined every inch of the kitchen and moved slowly up and down it. Compared to a typical dream, this complete lucidity thrilled me as always! I then turned to face my hands.

I managed to raise them, albeit it wasn't easy. They were quite normal, so why did I assume that I was so indolent? Additionally, I sensed a pressure above my right eye, leading me to believe that this could be my hand from when I dozed off on the right side. In this dream, I wanted to accumulate more. However, as time passed, things grew increasingly hazy, and I started to wonder about the unintended consequence of my wish. I instantly turned to glance around again, hoping to improve my vision, but everything remained hazy.

I slowly awoke when I turned to face my hands and felt the pressure return over my right eye. It was my hand that I was lying with my head crushed against it uncomfortably.

Achieving lucidity may also be hampered by certain deviances that may occur. However, when you achieve consciousness, you generally allow everything to remain inside a dream.

Although it hasn't happened often in my experience, I've heard from other lucid dreamers that the desire for sex can intensify significantly: I was with two guys and one woman at the same time. Throughout the lengthy dream, I spent a lot of time with the Japanese woman.

Once, while using a public restroom or bathroom, we conversed with one another till we unexpectedly collapsed and had a kiss. She removed her blouse and covered herself with a red bra. She enjoyed the color red because she wore red stockings and a panty.

To put it succinctly, I also became aware that I was dreaming, but I chose to ignore this lucidity and carry on with my sexual relations with this lovely Asian woman.

Once I regained consciousness in this dream, I let go of her again to complete the prior task. It is evident from this that lucid dreaming is highly driven and sensation-driven, and it can only be superseded by a more potent or less significant urge.

When you learn to practice this technique, many benefits and hours of entertainment come with living here. In these kinds of lucid dreams, sex is frequently very powerful, bordering on the ecstatic and intoxicating. But after that one lucid moment, I rarely allow myself to be distracted by my surroundings anymore. Furthermore, it is immediately seen that giving up on becoming conscious of this dream does not guarantee a better outcome because lucidity also entails ceding control of the ongoing process.

Errors might also occur when you are careless. The most notable and foolish of these occurred in the dream that followed, wherein, despite my subconscious's all too obvious cues, I just did not realize that I was dreaming:

In a dining area, I was seated with a few others. I had never heard of any of them. I presented a brief presentation about dreams after we talked about them. I informed them that everything might be a dream and that I could dream by walking into this dining room instead of waking up in a bed where dreams always begin. The audience gave a thoughtful nod, but the conversation soon veered off-topic. I tried again after that, but we could not reach a mutually beneficial agreement.

Upon awakening from this dream, all I could do was shake my head at my ignorance, as this brief lecture perfectly captured my being there since I was dreaming and had imagined it just this way. Though unaware of it then, I couldn't help but think of the others and how they could be so innocent, not thinking that the world may be a dream. This dream-naivety recurs frequently and ought to make one laugh instead of cry.

I promise that once a dream becomes clear, the mesmerizing clarity will remain with every dreamer forever. This is why being able to dream like this is highly sought after. It is possible, and many people have already experienced it, even though it is undoubtedly difficult to achieve and calls for numerous

recommendations and quick awareness
exercises.

Milton Keynes UK
Ingram Content Group UK Ltd.
UKHW050857210624
444436UK00014B/260

9 781835 733974